A Fruitful Death

A Fruitful Death

A BRIEF MEMOIR

In memory of
Wilhelmina Rouweler Downs
1936–2014

Stephen Downs

The quotes on pages vi and 97 are taken from *Our Greatest Gift: A Meditation on Dying and Caring* by Henri Nouwen (New York: HarperCollins, 1994).

The quotes on pages 18, 19, 34, 35, 49, 81, and 82 are taken from *Opening Doors Within: 365 Daily Meditations from Findhorn* by Eileen Caddy (Forres, Scotland: Findhorn Press, 20th anniversary edition, 2007).

The quote on page 82 is taken from the lyrics to the song "Do You Love Me?" from *Fiddler on the Roof*. Music by Jerry Bock, lyrics by Sheldon Harnick. 1964.

Cover photo: Wil Downs, 1968. Family photo.
Book design by The Troy Book Makers
Printed in the United States of America
The Troy Book Makers • Troy, New York • thetroybookmakers.com

To order additional copies of this title,
contact your favorite local bookstore
or visit www.tbmbooks.com

ISBN: 978-1-61468-306-3

Foreword

My wife Wil died of pancreatic cancer on December 17, 2014. This is a brief memoir about her illness and the last months of her life from March to December 2014, during which I sent out periodic updates to friends and family about her treatment progress and about the experience of dying. Enough people told me that these updates were helpful to them in their own encounters with death that I've decided to republish them in a more complete and accessible form. If they help anyone deal with dying or the death of a loved one, I am content.

I've arranged the passages chronologically, pretty much as I wrote them. A few sections were written in retrospect to fill in chronological gaps. Some entries are e-mails I sent or responses to e-mails I received. I've also included an extended preface, to introduce Wil to those who never had a chance to get to know her.

The title of this book is based on a quote from Henri Nouwen's book, *Our Greatest Gift: A Meditation on Dying and Caring*. His words were invaluable for both Wil and me throughout her illness:

Here is the most hope-giving aspect of death. Our death may be the end of our success, our productivity, our fame, or our importance among people, but it is not the end of our fruitfulness. In fact, the opposite is true: The fruitfulness of our lives shows itself in its fullness only after we have died. We ourselves seldom see or experience our own fruitfulness...But the beauty of life is that it bears fruit long after life itself has come to an end.

It is, of course, too soon to know what fruitfulness Wil's death will bring. But before she died she cleared a field of rich soil and fertilized it with her love. The seeds lie waiting for the spring to bring forth life again in the sun and rain of a new generation.

Stephen Downs
March 2015

Preface

I met Wil in 1966 while I was in the American Peace Corps in India and she was in the Dutch Peace Corps. She was born in 1936, grew up in a little Dutch town, Goor, near the German border, survived the German occupation of the Netherlands during World War II, and eventually became a nurse. Her region of Holland, Twente, was cozy and insular, with its own dialect and customs, and she treasured it. People who knew her expected that she would marry one of the local townsfolk and settle down to raise a family.

But Wil was different in many ways. She was fascinated by the bigger world outside of Twente—the "third world" that she had heard about but never seen. Having being raised in a devotedly Catholic home and taught by nuns for most of her schooling, she might have joined a Catholic mission overseas. But her open-mindedness warned her against trying to impose her religious values on others by going as a Catholic missionary. When President John Kennedy proposed the creation of the Peace Corps in 1961, the Netherlands was the first country after America to take up the idea, and in 1965 Wil had her chance to do something challenging abroad on behalf of her country rather than her church.

Wil was assigned to a local school health program in Lucknow, India. When the schools closed during the summer heat, the Dutch nurses were sent to an American Peace Corps youth camp in the Himalayas—where I had been assigned primarily to teach beekeeping. Wil knew very little English at the time, but we found ways to communicate. I later went back to law school in America and she went back to nursing in Holland. We kept in touch, she visited America in 1967, and eventually we were married in the Netherlands in 1968.

We raised three children: Margot, a teacher of English as a second language; Roger, an environmental advocate and lobbyist; and Philip, a Ph.D. public health specialist in neglected tropical diseases. Over the years, each married (Margot to Paul, Roger to Meredith, Philip to Jillian), and eventually Wil and I became grandparents: two grandchildren apiece from each of our children and their spouses.

When I first met Wil in India, the things that attracted me to her were her faith and compassion. She had the unusual combination of a strong faith within the Catholic tradition and an equally strong belief in the validity of other traditions. She intuitively understood the spiritual connectedness of all peoples of faith.

Wil was five and a half years older than I, with a wealth of practical experience when we met in India. She had survived the war years having seen some Jewish neighbors deported to death camps and other

Jewish neighbors hidden by Gentiles in the community. Her town had been bombed and half-destroyed. Her father had hidden in haystacks to avoid being conscripted into the Nazi war effort. During the hunger winter of 1945, when the west coast of Holland was starving, her family took in Dutch refugees and fed them until they were strong enough to return home with food for those too weak to make the trip.

After the war, Wil helped her parents raise their family of seven children. She went into nursing and experienced the death of children and the suffering of people living in poverty. Her faith was grounded in the reality of the human condition and produced in her a deep compassion.

From her experience, Wil understood that life was difficult and required discipline. Her two favorite sayings from that time were, "No pleasure before work is done," and "Mothers' work is never done." Fun was a guilty pleasure dispensed in teaspoons. She had been trained by fierce German nuns who preached cleanliness and constant hard work to avoid idleness. The experience taught her to keep a certain distance from the religious life, but her respect for the nuns' discipline never completely wore off. On occasion I jokingly called her "Our Lady, Queen of Perpetual Lamentations," and she would retort (with a certain gleam in her eye), "I am not like you, Mr. Enthusiasm. I don't need to celebrate every time I tie my shoelaces correctly. I am content. It is enough.

Don't ask for more." And by "content" I think she meant that she had done her duty: polished the house, manured the garden, pruned the children, improved her husband, entertained her friends, and attended to God. If it was not always fun, it was satisfying when done well, and left her feeling content.

My background was completely different. I grew up in the rich, white, WASPy town of Bronxville, New York. My grandfather, Harry Emerson Fosdick, was a well-known preacher and the founding minister of Riverside Church in New York City, which was financed by John D. Rockefeller, the richest man in the world at that time. It was my grandfather's vision to build a church that welcomed everyone and did not acknowledge any denominational divisions; a church that was active seven days a week to improve the lives of everyone, especially the poorest; a church that rejected fundamentalism and incorporated science and modern thinking into everything it did; and a church that staunchly advocated for peace. Almost a century later, I am pleased to discover that many of my progressive friends in New York City from all religious traditions and stations in life have been welcomed at Riverside, participated in its programs, used its resources, and still find it to be at the center of peace and justice debates.

But as a child, I found Riverside a bit overwhelming. With its grand Gothic nave, stained-glass windows, massive organ, carillon, professional-quality choir, and all the other amenities that riches could buy, it celebrated in style a mighty God enthroned above at the same time that it proclaimed a liberal acceptance of many worshiping traditions. As a child I could not find God there amidst all the pomp and pageantry, and it did not seem to be an authentic voice for the poor, either. At a time when I had little experience with the human condition, the dissonance between the style and the message made me uncomfortable, and I instinctively backed away.

My grandfather preached a liberal doctrine of the perfection of humans through the spirit of God, and this optimistic philosophy seemed to have permeated our family, from my mother to my sister and myself. We all tended to see the world through rose-colored glasses—we did not describe events in our lives as "disasters"; instead we had "adventures." Whatever did not kill us gave us strength. We did not lament our situation in life, but strove joyfully against the forces of evil (which fortunately often afflicted others somewhere else). I have heard my family described as "annoyingly cheerful" and "chronically in denial."

In 1945, when I was three years old, my father, a Navy doctor, died in the Second World War. Between 1948 and 1950, my mother, who was also a doctor, took my sister and me to live for two years in Geneva, Switzerland with the World Health Organization, perhaps as a way to participate in the rebuilding of Europe from the war that had killed her husband. As a junior in high school, I went as a foreign exchange student (through the American Field Service) to live with a family in New Zealand for eight months. Then, in the 1960s, my mother, who was by then working at New York's Columbia Medical Center and Harlem Hospital, sensed that I needed deeper experiences, because growing up in Bronxville was too white. "You need some blackness," she told me. She persuaded me to spend the summer after my freshman year at Amherst College in the Cameroon highlands of West Africa building a clinic with local tribesmen. A few years later, after I graduated from Amherst, this experience made it easy for me to join the Peace Corps and go to India.

When I met Wil in India, I had already been there for two years; she had been in India only one. And I had lived abroad far longer than she had, in a variety of different circumstances. But the lessons we had learned from our experiences were completely different. I saw my experiences as adventures; I did not see them as connected in any way to a religious faith, and I did not see the people I met, for whom I was now responsible, as gifts given to me. But Wil's experiences, coming out of the devastation of World War II, were compassionate expressions of solidarity with the poor and afflicted. It was the first time that I had encountered such compassionate faith, and I was attracted to it. Wil understood faith through the heart, while I could not understand it through the head. But it looked good on her, and I wanted to know more about it.

In time, Wil grounded my faith in compassion. Everything I know about compassion I learned from her. And I taught her that sometimes what God really loves is a good laugh. I could have fun in unconventional, unplanned ways that left her spluttering in indignation and amusement. We were good for each other.

Secretly I believe she loved my irresponsible, adventurous nature and at the same time felt it was her obligation to correct it and make me into a better person. I learned early on that when she started in on one of her "improvement lectures" the best response was to literally drop down on all fours and start hooting and scratching like a chimpanzee. Once when I did this on a street in Holland, a distinguished citizen passing by on his bicycle became so engrossed in the spectacle that he crashed his bike into a telephone pole. We used to joke that she had been sent as a missionary to the Americans to convert them to a normal lifestyle.

I often described Wil as the "least frivolous person I've ever met." She would cut up old plastic shopping bags into long thin strips and, while traveling, would knit them into beautiful colorful handbags so as not to either waste any discarded plastic or idle away the time riding in the car. She was an excellent artist, but had been told by her father that art was merely a passing pleasure that did not put food on the table. The only way she could bring herself to indulge in this guilty pleasure was to sign up for an art course that cost money, even though she might know far more than the instructor about the subject. Then she could say to her legion of hidden critics that it would be a sin to waste the money by not practicing painting daily for the course. The great love of her life was quilting, but she could only do it if the quilts were given away for charity or to family. In her world of rules and discipline, charity was acceptable only as long as you did not use it to show off.

Over the years she loosened up a little. She never was able to throw her head back and laugh a good belly laugh, but the hard edge of her discipline wore off a bit. And I learned that I could not develop as a human being without the compassion and responsibility that she modeled for me. We helped each other grow.

Wil's compassion led her to volunteer for hospice for many years. She helped people die, and in the process she taught me about dying. She would tell me about a bedridden client describing the angels circling around his room that only he could see, and she would predict that he would die by the weekend. She experienced toxic deaths that would poison relationships for generations to come, and she experienced fruitful deaths that gave friends and family spiritual nourishment in the years afterwards.

One of the ironies of cancer was that it challenged both our personalities. Every authority we consulted agreed that the success rate of any cancer treatment improved with a positive, upbeat personality. Wil was not blessed with such a personality; her glass was often half-empty. And I understood that I had to live in complete solidarity with her as she moved toward death, and to share her pain, even though compassion was not something I fully understood. In effect, the cancer required that we exchange personalities.

Wil had to learn to laugh at jokes—even bad jokes—and dream of a happy future even as the cancer progressed inside her. And when pain came to her in the night, I had to learn that sometimes the best response was to simply hold her, pray with her, and share her pain. When she needed something, it was infinitely more beneficial if I got it right away, because that told her I understood the urgency of her needs. We learned from each other.

In the end, I think our personalities meet in a sense of spirituality—the realization that all things, even opposites like death and life, are connected. There is a deep joy in this realization for both the irresponsible fun-lover and the disciplined compassionate one, and it was a place that the two of us, with such opposite personalities, could share as the cancer progressed.

A Fruitful Death

March 14, 2014

"I'm home." Wil sticks her head into the living room where I'm reading. "You won't believe what the doctor just told me." She disappears to deposit some packages in the kitchen.

What's going on with the doctor? I say to myself. *Oh, I remember. Wil had indigestion and went for a CAT scan. She got the results today. No big deal.*

She sticks her head back into the living room. "He says I have pancreatic cancer that has spread to my lungs. He says I have six months to live."

Dead silence in the room. I don't dare move or even breathe, because maybe if I am very quiet her words will go away and we can continue with our normal life. The clock ticks. The world does not end.

Finally I draw in a breath and go to the kitchen where Wil is putting away the packages. "What did the doctor say?" I ask very quietly.

"He said I have six months to live," she repeats. "Can you believe that! I have never been healthier. I feel fine. He said there's a tumor growing in my pancreas, and 'innumerable' spots on my lungs, and he just kept saying over and over 'I am so sorry, I am so sorry.'"

"Is he sure?"

"He said they would have to do tests to confirm, but he was pretty sure."

"And the six months?"

"No, he did not really say that. I asked him how long I had to live and he said maybe six months without treatment. But he is going to refer me to an oncologist who might be able to treat the disease with chemo."

I put my arms around her and hold her close, and from deep down inside me arises a huge sob, the biggest sob I have ever felt. It shakes my whole body for what seems like a long time. She holds me until the shaking stops and then she steps back and looks at me intently.

After forty-seven years of marriage, I've learned to read Wil's face. Words can be misunderstood, but eye contact is seldom wrong, and I know what she is telling me.

"I know you're afraid. I am afraid also. But I'm going to fight this cancer, and I need your support. You are no use to me if you're an emotional basket case. You have to be strong so we can deal with this together."

Suddenly I understand the role I will have to play. I dry my eyes, and it is the last time I'll cry outright until the end.

I've always known that Wil is a strong person, but I have never realized until now just how strong she is. Later in the day I begin to clear my calendar so that I'll be available for her whenever she needs me.

Late March and April

Wil's primary care doctor set up some appointments with members of the oncology team. The first person we saw was the surgeon, even though everyone agreed that surgery would not work for metastatic pancreatic cancer; surgery would only tend to spread cancer cells around the body.

Next, Wil had a biopsy of the tumor in her pancreas. The doctor who performed the biopsy told her in the recovery room that it was a very standard-looking cancer and said he believed that she had about six months to live. He was blunt about it, but the Dutch are often quite blunt themselves, and Wil appreciated his candor. His advice was for her to put her affairs in order as soon as possible while she still had the energy to do it.

We then had a meeting with the oncologist. He was very nice, but the opposite of blunt, and I wondered about his candor. He proposed treating Wil with Folfirinox, a cocktail of chemicals that he believed would extend her life by an additional six months. He seemed quite enthusiastic and confident about the treatment, but I kept hearing a warning voice in my brain: *He is not proposing a cure. He's talk-*

ing about getting another six months. Even if it works to perfection, he believes she will die in a year. This is a very desperate situation, and yet Wil doesn't look even look sick. She has always been in good health and she continues to look good. I cannot make sense of this.

We were prepared to start the chemo as soon as possible; already two weeks had passed from the time of the first diagnosis, and we felt that the earlier the treatment began, the better. But then we were told that the lung tumors first had to be biopsied to make sure they were cancerous. Nobody seemed to have any doubt that they were cancerous, but a biopsy still had to be done first before treatment could begin. I wondered why the biopsy could not have been done at the same time the pancreatic cancer was biopsied, but these concerns were brushed aside. So we had to wait until April 8 to have Wil's lungs biopsied and a port installed in her chest to infuse the chemo. More doctor visits were scheduled to recheck everything again, and it wasn't until April 23, five weeks after the first diagnosis, that Wil finally received the first chemo infusion. A delay of five weeks may not seem that long, but it was 20% of her expected six-month survival time. This weighed heavily on my mind as we waited.

In the meantime, Wil took very much to heart the doctor's instructions to "put her affairs in order" while she still had the energy to do it. We went to a lawyer and had our wills redone. Then Wil decided she wanted to interview funeral homes. The first place we visited was so old and disorganized that it seemed doubtful it had been cleaned in years. Even the plastic flowers were wilted. When we got in the car to leave, we both burst into laughter that such a place could exist. Eventually we found another funeral home that satisfied us. But I was grateful to that first funeral home, which provided us with such a heartfelt laugh at a time when we needed one the most.

Wil also visited a holistic treatment facility that provided integrative and supplemental treatments that focused on diet, acupuncture, vitamin C infusions, and other alternative therapies. Oncologists often do not like patients to take supplemental treatments while undergoing chemo because they fear that the supplements will interfere with their treatments. But our oncologist didn't object to most dietary treatments, only to vitamin C infusions. So Wil began a regimen of vitamins and minerals by means of dozens of pills a day designed to boost her immune system.

I decided to start sending out news updates to friends and family about Wil's health. With so many friends and family in this country, as well as in the Netherlands, it was a way to keep communication going. Wil's older sister, Regina, died of cancer several decades ago in Holland, and Wil had struggled to get news of what was happening, a frustrating time both for her and for her whole Dutch family. I know Wil's family very well, having exchanged many visits and adventures with them over the years, and I wanted to make sure that Regina's experience, compounded by language problems, was not repeated with Wil, and that her friends and family here and abroad felt included in her journey with cancer.

May 6

First health update

Hi friends and family—

Wil has had a rollercoaster ride the last few weeks. She received her first chemo treatment on April 23 and at first seemed to be sailing through it. She did not have any nausea or other bad side effects. Then four to five days after the chemo she developed serious mouth sores that made it almost impossible for her to eat unless she put everything in a blender and reduced the acidity. She was already on a highly restricted diet of no sugar (so as not to feed the cancer cells) and high protein (so as to build up her immune system) and no meat or dairy (so as not to cause inflammation in the body, which provides blood to growing tumors)—and now no acidic foods (so as not to inflame the mouth sores).

As a result of her difficulty in eating, she began to fall behind in her calorie and protein requirements. She also lost a lot of energy and was really dragging around. Then after a number of days, the mouth sores began to heal up, she began to eat more, and her energy improved.

The plan was for her to get treatments every two weeks, so yesterday she went back for an examination before her scheduled treatment on Wednesday—and the doctor discovered that her blood count (red and white blood cells) had crashed. He put her on a "vacation" from treatments until her blood count gets back to normal. He also said that he would reduce the medication so that she would not have these problems again. So right now we are on a treatment holiday for several weeks.

Wil›s energy is good in the morning and she enjoys such treats as cleaning her closets or clipping bushes. But in the afternoon she gets pretty tired. She is now eating well, and the mouth sores have healed up, but her hair is falling out. So it's a mixed bag. The biggest problem is that her immune system has taken a beating, and the doctor is advising her not to have visitors or go out in crowds until the system has rebounded in a few weeks. She loves to get cards and notes. Telephone calls are great if they're short. We both feel so blessed and grateful for all the love and support we have received. We believe that humor and optimism can help to boost the effectiveness of chemo, as can prayer and meditation.

Keep us in your prayers. We love you all.

June 7

Health update

Dear family and friends,

Wil is really doing pretty well, all things considered…they cut the chemo dosage by 30% and the subsequent two treatments have been pretty easy. She is tired and sleeps quite a bit, but when she's up she's gardening and writing notes and having visitors. The real question is whether the chemo is doing any good. We won't know the answer to that until the middle of August, when she's finished with six treatments and has been evaluated. So right now we have nothing to do but enjoy life to the fullest—admire the beauty of nature, hang out with friends, laugh, and pray.

June 19

Wil and I have just learned that a group of friends has decided to honor us with a Peace Pole. Although I don't know how they knew it, I have always loved Peace Poles and the Peace Pole movement. These are usually four-sided poles with the words "May Peace Prevail on Earth" written on each side in different languages. The poles are registered in a central registry, so that people can find their locations all over the world and can visit them. The poles publicly proclaim the desire for peace and suggest that the property where they're placed is a sanctuary for anyone seeking refuge (at least that's my interpretation of them). Wherever I've encountered Peace Poles, I have found people who are open to the world and to healing. I was delighted, for example, to find a Peace Pole outside of St. Peter's Hospital, where Wil has her chemo.

My feeling is that Peace Poles are not private property but rather expressions of community solidarity. An individual should not just purchase one; a pole should come from the community to express a sense of peaceful action that already exists. Our pole is being presented by a group of activists and humanitarians, each of whom has done far more than Wil or I to bring peace to the world, and so it's somewhat embarrassing to be honored by such a remarkable group of people. Why us? The answer, I think, is found in the languages on the pole that ask for peace on earth: English, Dutch, Vietnamese, Urdu, and Arabic.

Early in our marriage, Catholic Charities made an appeal for families to help resettle refugees. Wil and I volunteered, and in due course we helped resettle a Polish family, and later another individual from another Polish family. This was a wonderful experience, and we've remained friends with our "newcomers" ever since. At one point, while teaching religious education, I became friends with a Vietnamese refugee whose fourteen-year-old nephew, Hiep, had recently escaped Vietnam as a boat person and was being held in Hong Kong. My friend asked Wil and me if we would be a foster family for Hiep when he arrived in the United States. Hiep stayed with us for three years until he graduated from high school; he went on to Colgate University. Later, when Wil and I were in the Netherlands, we met an Iranian refugee family and sponsored them to come to the U.S. They stayed with us for several months, eventually moved into a house around the corner from us, and became close friends.

Through these four families, we came to know four remarkable children: Samantha, who has become a talented artist; Adam, who has become a Wall Street lawyer; Hiep, who has become a research chemist; and Shima, who has become an international architect. These children—talented, wholesome, focused, and positive—are our children as well, and have become very precious to us.

In 2003 I retired, after twenty-eight years, from my job as chief attorney for the New York State Commission on Judicial Conduct. In 2006, Wil got me involved as a volunteer lawyer in the terrorism trial of a local imam, Yassin Aref, who I was convinced was totally innocent. After he was convicted and sentenced to fifteen years, I became part of a new group, the Muslim Solidarity Committee, to take care of his four children and the six children of his co-defendant. The committee subsequently found other cases of Muslims who had been "preemptively prosecuted" based on suspicion rather than on criminal activity and formed another organization, Project SALAM (Support And Legal Advocacy for Muslims), to fight this corruption of the justice system. Project SALAM later became part of the National Coalition to Protect Civil Freedoms (NCPCF), and eventually I became its director. So these projects that Wil and I had undertaken over three decades were reflected in the languages and symbols on the Peace Pole.

I'm describing the Peace Pole in some detail because it has been one of several expressions of community support for Wil in her struggle against the cancer. When a person is told she has six months to live, there is a tendency to back away from the community and to go into seclusion. Why depress and embarrass people when they ask how you're feeling? But instead, Wil embraced the community and took enormous strength and energy from the people she loves. Part of a fruitful death is that it nourishes and enriches the entire community; Wil took this wisdom to heart.

June 29

We decided to "install" our Peace Pole on June 28, with the whole community invited. It seemed like one of those senseless, random acts of kindness that makes life so special. Unfortunately Wil's chemo treatments sent her to the hospital on June 27, and we had to do the event without her.

But the Peace Pole "conspirators"—friends and colleagues Jeanne Finley, Marwa Elbially, Lynne Jackson, and Kathy Manley—sent out a note to everyone who contributed to the pole to explain what happened and to describe its details and purpose:

> *We ordered a Peace Pole with four sides and eight "facets." The phrase "May Peace Prevail on Earth" is rendered in five different languages, to symbolize aspects of Steve and Wil's work for peace and justice: English, Dutch (for Wil, her native language), Urdu (for the area of India they both served in, in the Peace Corps), Arabic (for their commitment to the Muslim community), and Vietnamese (for the family they sponsored in the U.S.). In addition, there are footprints (for all the individuals they've helped), leaves (for*

Steve's and Wil's environmental work), and the phrase "May Peace Be in Our Homes and Communities"—which is our wish for them, on behalf of all of us. The Pole also has a small plaque attached, which reads:

For Steve and Wil
To honor your work for peace and justice
Thank you from your community
2014

July 1

Health update

Dear friends and family,

The plan had been for Wil to have six chemo treatments spaced two weeks apart and then evaluate the results. The fourth treatment started like all the others, with a period of three to four days when she felt fatigued. Normally this feeling would slowly subside over the next few days, but this time it did not, and Wil developed mouth sores again. Finally, on June 27, she was really dragging around, almost a week and a half after the chemo, and had the common sense to take her temperature. It was 101. She was admitted to the hospital, and after a lot of tests and consultations the doctors concluded that her blood count had crashed again. She had virtually no immune system left and had started to pick up infections, hence the fever. They immediately put her on intravenous antibiotics, and she will probably stay in the hospital for at least a week until her immune system has recovered and is functioning again. (The antibiotics are causing her severe diarrhea, which is uncomfortable but not really dangerous, since she's being infused with all sorts of liquids at the same time. It just goes in one end and out the other).

In the course of doing the tests, the doctors discovered today that after four treatments, the tumors in her lungs are still growing and expanding. The doctors said that the chemo treatment has been a failure, and they recommend stopping it. I think Wil and I both agree. Chemo has not been effective or palliative in her case; indeed, the chemicals damn near killed her.

Wil and I will explore instead things we can do to boost her natural immune system instead of killing it with chemicals. I think this approach will give her more quality time in a more holistic approach.

Eileen Caddy wrote a book of spiritual observations for every day of the week, called *Opening Doors Within*. Wil and I have for some time read her essays each morning as a way of starting the day on a good note. It happens that on July 1, today—the day that the doctors have decided the chemo has been a failure and should be discontinued—Caddy's essay seems remarkably on point. Wil and I were both touched by it.

> *Rejoice and give eternal thanks, for you know that you live forever. You do it one day at a time, living each moment fully and gloriously, forgetting the past, with no concern for the future, simply accepting that life is eternal and has no beginning and no end. All the time you are growing and expanding in consciousness, you are beginning to understand the mystery and wonder of life*

eternal and your realization of oneness with me, the creator of life. Step by step, you move onward and upward filled with peace, tranquility and serenity, realizing that as all is in my hands, you have nothing to concern yourself with. It is when you try to look too far ahead that life becomes a real burden, and too many souls bring fear, uncertainty and even lack of faith and belief. Become as a little child, free and joyous, and life will be a continual source of delight for you. Believe in life and live it fully.

July 3

An e-mail from Wil thanking everyone for the Peace Pole:

Dear friends,

You have touched my whole being so much by honoring Steve and me with this beautiful gift of the Peace Pole. I hope that you all feel honored as well because of all your effort to bring peace in the world and dedication to justice.

From my comforting hospital bed, I'm looking at the pictures you sent me. I wish I could have been there. Steve told me that you had such a good time.

I hope that whoever could not come will stop by someday and rest on the bench and meditate on Peace for every Nation on earth.

Peace to all. Wil

I also sent a note to all the contributors:

I want all of you to know how much we appreciate what you have done. This morning I showed all your notes to Wil. She had been too exhausted before to look at them. She was stunned. She just kept repeating with tears in her eyes, "I didn't know. I didn't know so many people cared." So many people from so many different groups and projects we had been, and are, involved with—it was pretty amazing. I'm really sorry Wil was not able to be at the Peace Pole installation party, but in a way I am glad it worked out like this. She really needed the emotional affirmation from all you wonderful people at this time (just like I do). Receiving such affirmation from all of you, whom I really love, respect, and admire, is the most precious thing I know. Thank you from both of us. Steve

July 6

I replied to an e-mail from Jeanne Finley, who talked about cancer as the "unwelcome visitor:"

Yeah—living with the unwelcome visitor. That's the perfect title for a book about cancer...and chemo. I think Wil is really glad to be home. She has spent almost all of a week in bed, so I shouldn't be discouraged if she doesn't just jump out of bed and start jitterbugging. We walked down to the Peace Pole and she really loved it—almost overwhelmed by the thoughtfulness of it—by the people who would do such a random act of kindness. I think for both of us it will always be a special spot because it embraces so many things our marriage has included— immigrants, peace, justice work. And in a way it points to a direction for dealing with cancer. If chemo is chemical warfare, a Peace Pole suggests another strategy. We'll see how things work out down the road, after (as we Catholics say) a period of discernment. Thanks for everything.

July 14

Health update

Hi everybody—

Wil has been out the hospital now for about a week and is slowly getting stronger, day by day. She still has signs of the chemo in her system, her taste is still messed up, and there are still nerve issues in her fingers, but each day I see steady small improvements. Her stamina is better; she can work longer in the garden; she eats better and is starting to get interested in food again. She draws such strength from all of you—her friends and family—and the prayers that you have made for her.

It is hard to tell how long she will continue to improve—how long it will take to get the harmful effects of the chemo out of her system. At some point I assume the reality of cancer will start to assert itself. But for the moment this is not something we have to worry about. What I love about this moment is seeing the old Wil back again, with a renewed joy in life, planning new gardens and quilts and surrounding herself with friends and family.

We are still not encouraging visitors (her immune system is questionable), and telephone calls can be sometimes difficult because the chemo also affected her already marginal hearing, but she loves notes and draws great strength from them. She actually rereads the notes from time to time, so one note goes a long way. Whatever the statistics may say, we continue to be optimistic about the future and we will look for healing in alternative ways that will not damage her body like the chemo treatment she received. Much love to you all.

July 27
Health update

Hi everybody—

We met with Wil's oncologist a week ago and he confirmed that the chemo was not stopping the cancer from spreading—indeed it was killing her by wiping out her immune system. He officially ended the chemo and we agreed that she should go into hospice. The doctor said that for about 20% of patients, chemo was ineffective against pancreatic cancer and actually might be counterproductive. Wil appears to be one such patient. He told her to go home and live life to the fullest—an interesting challenge on which I will comment more later.

Since stopping chemo, Wil's health has continued to steadily improve. Her thinking is clearer, her walk is steadier, her endurance and stamina are much better. She has no significant pain. In all respects she seems to be improving. The doctor said that the chemo might remain in her system for several months, so it seems reasonable to assume that her health might continue to improve for several months as she cleanses her system from the toxins.

You might ask, if Wil's health is improving, why is she going into hospice? The reason is that hospice is available to anyone whose has fewer than six months to live. When Wil was first diagnosed in March, the doctor estimated that number, and so she would have been a candidate for hospice then. However, we all hoped that the chemo would add an additional six months to her life, which would take her outside the six-months criterion. Now that the doctor has ended the possibility of chemo, the original estimate of fewer than six months has been reinstated.

But, you say, her health is improving! Why does she need hospice now? Wil was a hospice volunteer for ten years and she understands the system. Hospice is a great organization with an inspired mission, and the sooner a patient gets into hospice the sooner he or she can start to get the benefits from it, even if her health is temporarily improving. For example, hospice tries to keep patients in their homes for as long as possible. If modifications have to be made to do this, or extra equipment is needed, they can provide it. They can also help families go through the difficult transition from life to death, and can head off problems before they become overwhelming. All this takes time, and so the sooner a patient can get into hospice the better it is for her, even if there is no immediate crisis.

Hospice workers develop a special quality: a warm delight in people, a gentle acceptance of their situation in life, and a comfort with discussing spiritual matters. Or something like that. I once was on a plane, talking with the woman next to me, and I realized that she had this hospice quality. I said, "I'll bet you work with hospice." She said, "No, I'm an Army general." Then she said with a grin, "But I used to work with hospice." Once you have this quality, you don't lose it. Who wouldn't want such great folks in one's life as soon as possible?

In the meantime, Wil and I have been exploring an alternative treatment. In Europe there's a lot of interest in a theory called salvestrols (sal-VES-trols), but the theory is almost completely unknown here. One of Wil's Dutch nieces called our attention to it as soon as she heard about Wil's diagnosis. We looked around and found only one doctor in the Northeast who was using salvestrols. He was only about two hours away, in Suffern, New York, so we paid him a visit.

The theory of salvestrols is that the human body at any given moment has innumerable cancer cells floating around in it, and the body identifies them as damaged cells and destroys them as part of the normal human immune response. Cancer becomes a problem only when, for some reason, the immune response is suppressed or depleted for a period of time, allowing the cancer cells to take root, reproduce, produce tumors, and ultimately overwhelm the immune system's ability to kill them.

Researchers in England have found an enzyme called CYP1B1 (sip-one-be-one) that seems to be present only in cancer cells and not in healthy cells.

It is believed that this enzyme may represent the human immune response to cancer. The enzyme goes to cancer cells and brings in certain chemicals from the bloodstream that it can break down into toxic substances that will kill the cancer cells. These necessary chemicals in the bloodstream come from fresh ripe fruits and vegetables, which would have been present in abundance in the diet of early hunter-gatherers but may be lacking in the modern diet of processed foods. These necessary chemicals are salvestrols, and the point is to overload the body with salvestrols so that the enzyme CYP1B1 will have an abundance of resources with which to attack the cancer cells (but not the healthy cells). One cannot, of course, eat enormous quantities of fresh fruits and vegetables to overwhelm the body's immune system with resources. Instead, salvestrols have been extracted and reduced to highly concentrated food supplements in pill form.

In practice, it means taking an enormous number of pills, together with an equally large number of vitamins and minerals, to create the right conditions in the body to absorb and utilize these resources. Wil has some twenty-five pill jars lined up on the dining room table, ready to eat at each meal. In some ways it feels like a return to the old days, when everything revolved around chemo—except that in this case, the pills probably won't injure Wil's body or cause harmful side effects. All of this is quite expensive and is not reimbursed by insurance. Our initial visit resulted in the purchase of two large bags of pills costing some $1,500, good for about two months. (It sounds like a lot, and yet an uninsured fender-bender or lawsuit could cost at least that much. The chemo treatments cost more than $55,000, but of course that was covered by insurance.) We are planning to try the salvestrol theory for three months to see what effect it has on the cancer.

There are anecdotal stories about how effective salvestrols are, but no clinical trials have yet been done. (I think they are starting clinical trials in the UK, but we don't yet know the results). One might ask, why have no clinical trials have been started in the U.S.? Apparently someone has to pay for the trials, and salvestrols is a low-tech, relatively inexpensive way to treat cancer. Since nobody stands to make any money out of it, nobody is pushing for trials, and nobody wants to put up the millions of dollars necessary to do them. At least that's one explanation.

The doctor gave us a book called *Radical Remission*, about a study done on individuals who lived long beyond their predicted demise. The study found nine characteristics that all the individuals seemed to share:

1. Willingness to radically change their diet
2. Willingness to take control of their health decisions
3. Willingness to follow their intuition
4. Using herbs and supplements

5. Willingness to release suppressed emotions
6. Willingness to increase positive emotions
7. Embracing social support
8. Deepening spiritual connections
9. Having strong reasons for living

It's an interesting list, and it's gratifying to note that Wil seems to have all of the characteristics.

The ninth characteristic is particularly interesting because it hearkens back to our oncologist's suggestion that Wil go home and live life fully. What would a fully lived life look like? This last weekend, Wil's niece, Claudia, was visiting from the Netherlands with her husband and three children. My sister and her husband and my foreign exchange Turkish "sister" were also visiting from Boston, along with my real sister's daughter and her husband from Kingston. Wil's brother was also visiting from the Netherlands, and our daughter Margot was visiting from Maine. So we had a house full of people. During the course of the weekend people from hospice dropped by, and friends and neighbors came calling. We ended up with three donated cakes, two of which were promptly eaten. At various times Wil became very tired and went up to bed, so visitors brought food and prepared meals. Others weeded the garden. The kids were entertained with trips. There was discussion and laughter. So much was going on that we pretty much forgot about the cancer for awhile.

At one point Wil and I looked at each other and said, "Wow, this is pretty busy and intense. Does it make sense for us to be doing all this right now?" But we concluded that if it was tiring and intense, it was also wonderful. It was life lived fully, with friends and relatives sharing their own pains and joys, rather than leading lives centered around ourselves and the cancer only.

We will try as long as possible to not let the cancer define and isolate us from our friends and family, and to be open to all of you. Bear with us if we forget to respond, or do not always express appreciation for all you do to support us. We really do appreciate and love you all, and we believe that in a deep spiritual way it is this connection with all of you that is keeping Wil alive and vital.

September 8
Health update

Hi everyone,

Wil has been off chemo for about three months, and she has been on the holistic salvestrols treatment for about one month. It takes four to six months to judge the effectiveness of salvestrols (which boost the human immune response to kill cancer cells), and so we just have to be patient before deciding if the holistic approach will work for her. On the other hand, she's been gradually gaining strength as the chemo leaves her body. She is now pretty much chemo free, and in a position where her main struggle is with the cancer and not with the chemo.

The good news is that she's doing well for someone in hospice. The universal reaction of the doctors and nurses who see her is, "Wow. You're doing well. You're doing *really* well." When you meet her, you might not know anything was wrong. She eats well and is keeping her weight up. She sleeps well. She holds animated conversations and enjoys her friends and family.

But the bad news is that she struggles to do these otherwise normal activities because of two significant problems: lack of energy, and pain. The lack of energy is seemingly always with her. An hour or so of conversation tires her out. A walk upstairs or to the mailbox leaves her breathing hard. She has good days and bad days, but lack of energy is always present to some degree. We assume that the cancer has reduced the efficiency of her lungs, depriving her of some oxygen.

Blood oxygen saturation for most people is around 98% or 99%, and if you fall below 90% you're entering the problem zone. Wil's oxygen level hovers around 90%—sometimes a little above and sometimes a little below. A few days ago, hospice delivered some tanks of oxygen; this has improved her energy. Her saturation level is now regularly up to 92% and she seems a little more vigorous.

Wil has also been experiencing a moderately strong ache deep inside her ribcage, which is probably from the lung cancer, and back pain when she lies down, which may be from the pancreatic tumor pressing on some nerves. The pain can be managed with drugs such as Tylenol or ibuprofen, but these drugs may conflict with the holistic approach. Modern medicine tends to say, "If you're experiencing pain, take a drug that will prevent you from feeling the pain." The holistic approach says, "If you're feeling pain, take natural substances that will help your body heal itself so that the cause of the pain will go away." The idea is not to mask a particular pain, but to give the body what it needs to heal itself and function at its optimal level.

Our holistic (alternative) doctor recommended that Wil give up ibuprofen and use willow bark extract, which may chemically be related to aspirin. The problem is that the willow bark doesn't really control the pain as completely as ibuprofen. So when you're really hurting and in deep pain, how holistic do you want to be? This will have to be negotiated.

A related problem is that Wil's blood pressure has been fluctuating, and at times gets very high, which causes her to feel lousy. (It may have something to do with the low oxygen level in her blood). For years she used a common drug, Verapamil, to control her blood pressure, but now the doctor is recommending that she give up Verapamil and control her blood pressure with celery seed extract. We are about to go to her primary care doctor and explain that because her blood pressure is going up, we're replacing Verapamil with celery seeds...I expect his eyes will cross. But when you're in hospice, nobody can refuse you anything; you are medically free to experiment and have as many adventures as you want.

My favorite guru, Eileen Caddy, had this remarkably apt advice for September 6:

> *Live one day at a time. Do not try rushing ahead making plans for tomorrow, for tomorrow may never come. Enjoy today to the full; enjoy it as if it were your last. Do all the wonderful things you have longed to do, not recklessly or thought-*

lessly, but with real joy. Be like a small child who takes no thought for tomorrow and has forgotten what happened yesterday, but just lives as though the only time that matters is now. The now is the most exciting time you have ever known, so do not miss a second of it. Live on the tips of your toes, ready for anything to happen at any moment. When you live this way you are ready and open for anything that may take place. Changes will come and they will come very quickly. Lift up your heart in deep gratitude as they come along one by one. Always see the very best in every change that takes place.

September 16
Health update

Hi everybody—

I just wanted to send a quick update to my last e-mail. The oxygen has turned out to be a big help. After using it for several days, Wil's oxygen saturation level moved up into the mid-90s and her heart rate went down, along with her blood pressure. In retrospect it seems clear that her lungs were not absorbing enough oxygen, and so her heart was pumping harder to get oxygen to the cells, and as a result her blood pressure was going up. Now, with more oxygen coming in, her body can relax a little. (The connection is so obvious I'm embarrassed I didn't see it earlier; I tend to look at each of these symptoms as a separate issue).

Because it may take months for the salvestrols to become effective, we wondered if there was anything else we could do in the meantime. It turned out that there was one other thing that our alternative doctor recommended: vitamin C infusions.

Wil and I had been resisting vitamin C infusions because that seemed to be a return to the "chemo" approach of killing cancer cells with a foreign substance rather than with the body's natural immune system. However, vitamin C clearly does not harm the healthy cells the way chemo does. Since it is able to target only cancer cells, we decided to give it a try.

Yesterday was Wil's first vitamin C infusion. We drove two hours—with a certain amount of apprehension—to the center on the New Jersey border where the infusions were administered. We remembered what had happened the last time Wil was infused. But although the infusion unit looked and operated just like the chemo infusion unit in Albany, the atmosphere was completely different. The patients in the chemo infusion unit tended to feel sick and depressed. Nobody talked, and the room was as quiet as a...well, as a tomb. But in the vitamin C infusion unit, the patients were feeling better and they liked to talk. We met a lot of new friends and people seemed to want to share their stories. It was almost a party atmosphere, with a lot of laughter.

On the way home Wil was feeling good, so we decided to take a detour across the Hudson to get some fruit at our favorite orchard. On the way we got completely lost. Just when it seemed that we would never escape from the winding and endless back roads of Columbia County, we miraculously ended up at the orchard by means of a by-lane I had not known existed. We bought apples for the winter and Wil bought nectarines for a nectarine pie. Then we stopped at an antique store and bought an inexpensive painting of Monhegan Island. When we got home we walked around the outside of the house and marveled at the glory of Wil's garden at the end of summer, and ended up sitting on the stone bench in front of the Peace Pole. Simultaneously we turned to each other and said, "Wow—this was a really good day." And I think by "a good day" we meant that it was a day in which we were not defined by cancer. We met some new friends, we had a little adventure, we made some plans for the future, we bought some food and something special to look at, and we felt the beauty of the season and remembered the love of our community. Truly, days like this are really good.

People have been experimenting with vitamin C for half a century, after double Nobel Prize winner Linus Pauling promoted vitamin C as a cure for just about everything, including the common cold. Over the decades certain "facts" about vitamin C seem to have been generally accepted by scientists. (And here I am condensing some dense and contentious discussions about vitamin C into what I think is true and relevant, but I may be oversimplifying to some extent):

> 1. At low to moderate concentrations, vitamin C is not harmful to the human body and has virtually no side effects, except in rare cases.
>
> 2. At high concentrations, vitamin C produces/induces something toxic (perhaps hydrogen peroxide), which tends to kill cells.

3. Cancer cells absorb/concentrate vitamin C to a much greater extent than healthy cells. (It is one of the few substances to show this concentration property specific to cancer cells.)

This unusual ability to concentrate vitamin C in cancer cells allows a cancer therapy in which high doses of vitamin C are administered in such a way that the amount of the vitamin concentrated in the cancer cells is lethal, while the lesser amount concentrated in healthy cells is not. Vitamin C therapy is thus about the only therapy, other than salvestrols, to target cancer cells without killing healthy cells.

Anecdotal experience suggested that the theory worked, and so a number of years ago a study was undertaken to determine if vitamin C was the miracle cancer drug it appeared to be. Cancer patients were fed high dosages of vitamin C to see if it would prolong their life beyond the average cancer patient's life expectancy. At the end of the trial it was determined that there was no difference between the two groups; vitamin C had failed the test. This should have been the end of vitamin C as a cancer treatment, and for mainstream scientists it was. However, experimentation and treatment with vitamin C continued "underground."

Recently researchers found that the definitive test of years ago was probably invalid. The patients were fed high doses of vitamin C by mouth. At the time it was known that vitamin C was readily absorbed from the stomach into the bloodstream at low concentrations, but apparently it was not appreciated that at high doses the absorption rate was much lower. Recalculating the effect of the high oral doses given to the test patients indicated that the absorbed concentration of vitamin C in their blood wouldn't have been high enough to kill the cancer cells.

Researchers found that the absorption problem could be avoided by administering vitamin C intravenously, so that the concentration in the blood would be made much higher and more closely controlled. Suddenly vitamin C infusion became a popular alternative approach to cancer treatment.

I give you this background because if you ask doctors about it, you will get a range of opinions all the way from "It's just one of those frauds that has to be disproved every few years" to "Vitamin C should be used to complement every cancer treatment." Opinions and facts about vitamin C are all over the map.

Wil and her fellow nurse and friend, Nini Timmers, ca. 1960.

Family photo

41

Wil on our wedding day,
August 27, 1968.

Family photo

Wil and I leaving on our honeymoon to Ireland, 1968.

Family photo

Wil and her two living sisters, Josephine (Jos)
and Maria (right), ca. 2000.

Family photo

Wil's quilting group, The Piece Makers. From left:
Eileen Pasquini, Mary George, Carmen Bermudez, Wil.

Family photo

Four generations of the Downs clan celebrate our 45th wedding anniversary in Maine in 2013. Top row adults: Paul (Margot's husband), daughter Margot, Meredith (Roger's wife), son Roger, me, Wil, Jillian (Philip's wife), son Philip. Bottom row adults: our "adopted" nephew Hiep, and "Omi" (Dutch for "grandma"), my mother, Elinor, age 102.

Family photo

The installation of the Peace Pole, June 28, 2014.

Photo by Good Angel

Wil's entire family (American and Dutch) in front of her church in Goor, Netherlands, for her memorial service, May 3, 2015—the same church where she was baptized and where we were married.

Family photo

October 17

Health update

Dear friends and family,

Wil's health has taken a turn for the worse. She's been having more bad days than good days, and we feel that things are not progressing well. A recent blood test indicated that her "necrotic" index (the index of the extent to which cells are dying) was low, suggesting that few cancer cells were being killed, and her "inflammation" index (indicating the extent of inflammation in her system) was high, suggesting that the cancers (which cause inflammation) were still aggressive. This aggressiveness in turn appeared to lead to more pain, which over a long period of time is exhausting.

Wil had been on ibuprofen to combat the pain, but recently ibuprofen was not able to get the job done by itself, so last week she reluctantly went on morphine to supplement the ibuprofen. Together they did a really good job of pain relief, and so over the last week the pain has receded into the background as an issue. Instead, it has been replaced by exhaustion.

We found that Wil's blood oxygen level was low, at times as low as 85%. Presumably this is caused by the aggressive lung cancer, which occupies more of her lungs and leaves less room for breathing. When the oxygen gets that low, Wil feels really tired and is unable to function normally. We have been trying to relieve this problem with an oxygen tank, but increasingly the extra oxygen is just not able to compensate. Even simple things like walking and talking become a struggle on occasion, even with extra oxygen.

We've started twice-a-week massive infusions of vitamin C at the Alternative Center, about fifteen minutes from our house, which we hope will be able to reverse or at least check the cancer's aggressiveness. The center has been really great to us, but like salvestrols it will take some time for the vitamin C to work, and time is running out.

Cancer has a way of compressing reality down into days and hours and minutes. Nothing seems quite as important as the moments in which you are alive. Even simple things take on an outsized significance. A few weeks ago Wil asked me if she should order more spring bulbs. Sensing an existential issue underneath the question, I said that tulips are still beautiful even if the planter is not there to see them. She said, "Exactly!" and went on to order over 350 bulbs. As she's been getting slowly weaker, we have spent time outside planting the bulbs. After we finished planting the last one, Wil said to me, "There. Now I have to live to spring to see them all bloom." So spring has become the new horizon.

Recently, as I was looking out over Wil's glorious garden (and glorious is the only fitting word for it), I was struck by how vividly the flowers were blooming. These flowers must in some biological way know that in a few days a killing frost will leave them all wilted and dead. Trees know to drop their leaves before winter; tomato and squash plants know to produce fruit well before the cold sets in. But these last zinnias, dahlias, and mums seem to be trying to put on one last grand show before the end comes. I am tempted to ask why. What possible good will it do them to bloom so exuberantly in the face of certain annihilation? But that is the pattern—one generation passing on beauty, determination, and resilience to the next, guided through the dark winter by that spirit of love and life that animates us all.

My favorite guru, Eileen Caddy, had this to say today:

> *All things are part of the perfect whole, and everything you do, say, think, and feel is part of it. Therefore do not limit yourself in any way but feel yourself expand and expand, taking in more and more. You will never reach the limits because there is no limit. Life is infinite and you are part of that infinity.*

October 25

Health update

Dear friends and family,

On October 22, a group of friends and parishioners organized a healing service for Wil and me. Our former pastor, John Kirwin, presided, and some eighty or more friends were present. The service included singing, laying on of hands, anointing with oil, prayers, and lighting candles. (There were so many candles that Wil turned off her oxygen to avoid blowing up the building.) Each person was given a tulip bulb to take home and plant, and a candle to light. Wil was given several beautiful prayer shawls knitted by parishioners, and we included another cancer patient, Helene Conroy, in the service.

I cannot express the delight I felt at seeing so many friends from so many faiths and backgrounds all coming together for an evening of prayer with us. When they laid their hands on my head I felt a deep warmth envelop me all the way down to my feet. The experience of love and prayer was so intense it almost seemed physical, like a warm embrace. It was deeply moving and quite overwhelming for both of us. This intense feeling of being unconditionally loved has stayed with me long after the service, and hopefully it will stay forever. Later I thought of how many people, who must have illnesses even worse than Wil's, do not have this kind of community support that helps you believe anything is possible. It's a reminder to be more mindful.

A few weeks ago I caught Wil at one of her secret pleasures: reading a book of prayers by Mother Teresa. Wil confessed that her favorite prayer is the last one in the book:

> *Lord, renew my spirit and draw my face into smiles of delight at the richness of your blessing.*
>
> *Daily let my eyes smile at the care and companionship of my family and community.*
>
> *Daily let my heart smile at the joys and sorrows that we share.*
>
> *Daily let my mouth smile with the laughter and rejoicing in your works.*
>
> *Daily let my face give testimony to the gladness you give me.*
>
> *Thank you for this gift. A*men

I think Wil is drawn to this prayer because in a time of hardship, pain, and fear it is sometimes difficult to smile and be grateful. Mother Teresa's prayer is as much a challenge as a prayer. Can you rejoice, laugh, and sing at a time of suffering and decline? When the doctors decided that there was nothing more they could do for Wil, they sent her home to "live life to the fullest in the time that remains." We are starting to realize a "full life" must include gratitude and joy. So we try to sing one song every morning and to practice laughing at things that can be laughed at, in order to see the world in a more positive light. It is a learning experience.

Every day we meet such wonderful people and experience such love and acceptance that we feel very fortunate. The prayer service was again a reminder of this. There will be tough times ahead if Wil's health continues to deteriorate, but we know that we will never have to face it alone. We are loved and supported.

I have to conclude with one more story about Wil's complete dependence on flowers. On Wednesday, she announced that she wanted to clean out the basement. After fifteen minutes without oxygen she emerged gasping but triumphant, with two boxes of stuff that she was ready to give to the local flea market. To my surprise she insisted on accompanying me to the flea market, oxygen tank and all. At the market she approached the owner and locked eyes with him in a steely gaze. "The usual?" she said.

He nodded, "The usual," and turned away.

What on earth was this all about? I asked myself.

I trailed behind her, completely mystified, as she marched to the back of the store, where on a shelf of glass containers she found two hyacinth vases that could be used to force hyacinth bulbs in the winter to flower. "The usual" was code for a trade—one vase for each box of junk, in order to have hyacinths blooming in winter to lift the darkness. As long as there are blooms, there is hope.

November 7

Health update

Friends and family,

Wil's health has continued to slowly decline over the last few weeks. She still has good days and bad days—and, increasingly, good hours and bad hours—but overall the disease seems to be progressing in the short term. We still hope that in the long run the salvestrols and vitamin C infusions will make a significant difference, but at the moment it is hard to say what effect they are having, except perhaps to slow the spread of the disease.

The two devils that have been tormenting Wil, fatigue and pain, have been joined by two other devils, nausea and coughing, to make life very difficult at times. A full stomach of food seems to put pressure on the pancreatic tumor, causing nausea. We have learned that Wil has to eat small snacks every few hours rather than three big meals. Even so, she has been losing weight and needs to eat more. The doctors and nurses tell us that pain, fatigue, nausea, and coughing are all familiar and normal symptoms of pancreatic cancer. We have to deal with them as best we can.

This Thursday was a good example of the kinds of challenges and triumphs we've been living with. Wil coughed all night, got little sleep, and was exhausted when she got up in the morning. She was so weak that she almost collapsed and seemed to be in considerable distress. But she couldn't go back to bed because we had an appointment in the morning with the oncologist/hospice doctor, and another appointment in the afternoon for a vitamin C infusion.

Doctor visits have become more difficult because we have to take oxygen, snacks, and papers with us and walk to the doctor's office at a time when Wil may feel exhausted. Also they waste a lot of time and don't seem to accomplish much. For example, when Wil asked if they could do an X-ray to determine if the disease was progressing, the doctor shrugged and said, "It's obviously progressing. Why would you want an unnecessary medical procedure to document something we're not going to do anything about anyway? That's why you're in hospice." He was right, of course, but it was not exactly the response we were looking for.

When we got back from the vitamin C infusion at about 4 p.m., we felt like we had put in a full day. But vitamin C infusions always seem to provide an energy boost for Wil. Suddenly she decided it was time to work on the "office-to-bedroom" project. The first floor back room has always been designated as Wil's "office," and over the years it had filled up with files, papers, books, and all kinds of other stuff. We decided to put in a bed so she could easily take naps during the day without having to go upstairs. But she insisted that the room first had to be cleaned up, and she never seemed to have the energy to do it. (Who has?) Yet on Thursday she plunged into the room and began throwing out papers for some two hours.

After about an hour, she stuck her head out and said she was too busy, that I should make supper. Making supper is a complicated matter, because Wil has no appetite and it is not clear at any given moment what she will eat. So I decided to play "Freezer Safari," in which you go to the deepest, darkest, most remote corner of your freezer and see if you can find any critters hiding there that might make a tasty meal. Sure enough, I found several meals that we had been unable to finish and had frozen. Defrosted and put in separate bowls, they made perfect dishes to snack from, and when Wil was finished snacking I ate the rest. We cleaned up the kitchen and went off to do our e-mails.

Eventually, when I went upstairs to tuck Wil into bed, I saw she was reading Henri Nouwen's *Our Greatest Gift: A Meditation on Dying and Caring*. She smiled up at me and said, "I feel so much at peace." It reminded me of the hymn we sing in church:

> *Healer of our every ill, light of each tomorrow.*
> *Give us peace beyond our fears, and hope beyond*
> *our sorrow.*

November 15

Health update

Dear friends and family,

On Wednesday the hospice nurse, Sheila, confirmed what had become obvious over the last few weeks: Wil's body is shutting down. Sheila explained that the cancer was expanding aggressively and taking most of the nutrients in Wil's body to fuel its growth. In response, the body shuts down, suppressing appetite and refusing to process food. This is normal and typical of pancreatic cancer. Sheila said that it was counterproductive to try to force-feed someone under these conditions—food will just accumulate and become a problem. It was better to let the patient "listen" to her body and eat as little or as much as she wanted.

The result has been that Wil is eating only very small amounts—a few spoonfulls of soup here, some oatmeal there. Often she is nauseous. Many generous people have cooked food and soup for us, but Sheila's prediction is already coming true: the food, uneaten, is backing up in the kitchen and threatening to overwhelm our freezer capacity. At this point we have enough food to last for months. I am the beneficiary of all this generosity, but we have more than enough.

In the same way, Wil's lung capacity seems to be decreasing. Raising her oxygen levels in the oxygen condenser doesn't help much because her lungs are so congested that the oxygenated air cannot circulate. The result is that Wil is exhausted much of the time and sleeps for long periods. It has been increasingly difficult for her to spend time with visitors because talking and listening require considerable energy, which she just does not have at this point.

Wil told our daughter, Margot, that it was frustrating not to be as active as she was only a few weeks earlier. Margot suggested that we try something different—like dancing. It seemed like an implausible suggestion at the time. But a few days ago I saw Wil looking tired and reached to give her a hug. Instead of hugging back, she put her arms around me and began to sing, "I could have danced all night." So we slowly waltzed around the room, singing and trying to avoid tripping over her oxygen cord, until finally her gasping suggested that we stop. These are the special moments that keep alive a quality of life at a time when the horizon of possibilities is rapidly shrinking. We have found back massages are also a good method of communicating feelings for which words are inadequate.

I used to think that life and death were opposites. You were either alive or you were dead. But I'm discovering that the line between life and death is fuzzy and blended. Sometimes in the silence of the bedroom

I sit and watch Wil while she's asleep. It is a very active sleep. Her hands move in graceful gestures of picking a flower or caressing a cheek, and her lips move in silent communication. When she wakes, I ask her, "Who were you talking to?"

"You mean the hand gestures? It is funny—I just started doing them recently and I don't know why. I don't remember who I am talking to. Just people, I guess—nice people, but I don't know who they are."

Sometimes while watching Wil, I think I hear the whispering of voices in the room: "We are ready when you are." "Take your time, there is no rush." "We are expecting you." I suppose it's just a trick of the brain—the swish of the oxygen pump in the silence of the room that creates the whisperings I hear—but they comfort me.

Some years ago, Wil's mother died. A few months later Wil woke me up in the middle of the night, all excited. "I just spoke to Mom," she said. "I heard the telephone ring and it was Mom calling to say that she was thinking of you and me and that she loved us. I said, 'Mom—you can't talk to me. You are dead.' And Mom said, 'What do you mean? Just because I am dead doesn't mean I cannot talk to you!' And then I woke up."

Again, perhaps this dream was just a trick of the brain. Perhaps when a person dies there's nothing left, as though the person never existed; or perhaps death is the soul breaking free from a body that can no longer contain it. It is not important for me to know the answer right now. All humans who have ever existed have died, or will die. Death is completely natural and not something to fear. For the moment, it's enough to know and feel the possibilities—to see Wil silently speaking in her sleep, and hear the gentle whispers in reply.

Dear friends and family,

Wil's health has continued to slowly decline, although she still has good days and bad days. She now spends much of her time in her downstairs bedroom sleeping, balancing her checkbook, and doing e-mail. She is unable to eat much, and nausea and pain are frequently present. Her energy level is so low that it is very difficult to have visitors. Instead we are encouraging "companions" to stay with her when I have to go out. (Companions are able to simply be present even when Wil is sleeping and do simple things around the house that help save Wil's energy for when it's really needed.)

A few days ago I had to go to a Civil Liberties Union meeting and asked a friend to stay with Wil until I got back. When I returned, I asked the friend how it went. The friend replied that little had happened: Wil had slept most of the time, and the friend had just read a book, tidied up the room a bit, removed some dead flowers, and washed a few dishes. After the friend left, Wil woke up. I asked her how it went with our friend. "Oh, she was excellent!" Wil said. "She knew exactly what had to be done."

At the CLU meeting, another friend slipped me a twenty-page hospice booklet entitled *When Death Is Near: A Caregiver's Guide*. It was perfect for what I needed. In non-technical language it described the physical stages that people often go through when they die, and suggested simple things that a caregiver could do to help. Signs of approaching death include:

1. Withdrawal from friends and family; spending hours in bed sleeping; less verbal communication.

2. Lack of interest in food; nothing tastes good.

3. Changes in breathing; body temperature fluctuating.

4. Confusion and disorientation; use of symbolic language, such as wanting to "go home" when the person is already at home.

5. Restlessness and agitation; less oxygen reaching the brain; unfinished or unresolved issues that keep a person from being at peace.

6. Surges of energy. Some advice from the book on this one: "Enjoy this time for what it is; use the time to reminisce and say good-bye; be together holding hands."

I finished reading the pamphlet in about fifteen minutes and gave it to Wil, who read it also—surprisingly carefully. We recognized ourselves in many of the passages. If the vitamin C infusions and salvestrols are unable to check the progress of the cancer, we will have to start looking at the final stage of dying. We held hands because she was too tired to say much.

One of the topics in the book was how to say goodbye. It suggested starting sentences with "What I loved most about you…"; "I will always remember that you…"; "What I learned from you…," etc. These are good ways to begin. But at a time when verbal communication is so difficult, sometimes non-verbal communication can be more important. I have come to understand that my becoming a caregiver, the role that Wil always had, is in a sense a non-verbal way of my affirming the values that Wil has exemplified. If my actions show my appreciation for all that she did for so many years, elaborate words to her may not be necessary. And Wil, by gradually letting go and turning over to me work that she used to do, is affirming her confidence in my ability to carry on by myself. We understand, I think, what each of us means, and for the moment it is sufficient.

Next week is Thanksgiving. We have much to be thankful for, in particular all of you. We also know that when the whole family is together we will need to spend time gently talking with each other about the future and what is to come. And with six young grandchildren, it will also be a time to explain and educate about death and the meaning of life in a gentle, loving way that is reassuring and not fearful. This may not be easy to do.

Keep us in your prayers.

December 2

Health update

Friends and family,

Before Thanksgiving I was concerned about how everybody, including our six little grandchildren, would be able to understand what was happening to Wil and say goodbye. I felt a need to control the narrative, but I had no idea what to say about death and dying. However, events unfolded in an unusual way. Two days before Thanksgiving, our son Roger and his wife Meredith called to say that their dog had been hit by a car and killed. He was an unusually intelligent and engaging dog, and his death was a big shock to everyone. Then, after the Thanksgiving meal, one of the grandchildren developed severe cramps and pains in the stomach and had to be taken to the emergency room. So there were discussions about death and pain during Thanksgiving, but they just did not directly involve Wil.

What really happened was that Wil spent much of the time in her back bedroom, and our children and grandchildren stopped by from time to time to hang out. The older grandchildren brought her food and medicine, and the younger grandchildren told her what was going on in the rest of the house or drew pictures for her. One grand noticed that Wil didn't have a doll to play with, and gave Wil her doll. (Wil promptly fell asleep and slept for some time with the doll in her arms).

Wil was able to read stories to the kids and talk about their drawings. What I realized was that the grandkids didn't want or need a scientific explanation of dying. They intuitively understood that something serious was happening to their grandmother and wanted to be with her to understand it. It was very touching to see how gently they treated Wil, and how lovingly Wil treated them. Saying goodbye seemed less about finding the right words than about feeling comfortable with death as a natural process—the last stage of life— and being willing to let go without regrets.

I just realized that it has now been almost nine months since Wil was diagnosed with cancer. It is as though we've been going through a pregnancy for a new life together, and in a few weeks will come the labor as she is rebirthed. I also have to be ready to say goodbye, to let her go and not hold her back from her new journey.

Each week Wil's energy level seems to slip a little lower, as though she's been given a battery with enough power for one hour at low speed or half an hour at high speed. If she does the laundry or talks with visitors, she has a half-hour. If she reads or does her e-mail, she may last an hour. But when the energy runs out, her eyes just close and she goes to sleep until the battery is recharged.

And then sometimes she gets a sudden burst of energy that can go in any direction. Once she woke up and said, "This is no life for me." I said, "OK, what do you want to do?" She replied, "I want to play Scrabble!" So we played Scrabble. On another occasion I came in and found her sprawled awkwardly on the floor. I exclaimed, "What can I do to help?" Gasping for air, she forced out the words, "Stop helping! I am doing yoga!"

Recently she's been focused on tying up loose ends. Many years ago I took a trip to Mali with our son Philip, and before I left Wil insisted that I write out my obituary and funeral service—just in case. So now Wil and I are talking about what to put in her obituary and her funeral service—just in case. (She wants to exit the funeral to the song, "When the Saints Go Marching In.")

When she gets a burst of energy she often cleans out a desk drawer or a filing cabinet. One challenge so far has been to get her checkbook balanced. It's like Zeno's arrow: each time she tries, she gets halfway closer to the bank's total, and so logically she could spend the rest of her life trying to get to the bank's total and never quite hit the target. But this does not stop her from spending hours, half-asleep, adding and subtracting the debts.

The biggest unfinished project is to complete her "memoirs." She's determined to write something so that her grandchildren will know a little about their Dutch roots. She was going to do it all herself, but as time has slipped away she has less and less energy for the project, so I've been helping to fill in some gaps and get the writing tidied up. I give her some type-written pages, and she summons up enough energy to mark them all up with corrections. We've just arrived at the point in our lives when we were married. I think we will stop there. It is enough.

Recently Wil was telling me how wonderful it was to get letters and e-mails from so many friends. It reminded her of all the fun they had shared together. But then she said it was hard to imagine sharing these wonderful times in the future. It was as though she was starting to break her attachment to her connections on earth. Family members and friends who had died seemed to be coming closer to her, she said, and she thought often about them. Then, without breaking stride, she looked sharply at me and said in her best Mother Superior tone, "By the way, that plant isn't getting enough water. Make sure that you water it."

I laughed out loud and said, "Hey, I thought you were breaking your earthly attachments."

"I love it when you laugh," she said, and then added with a twinkle in her eye, "Are you in denial?"

"Death is natural," I said. "I'm just trying to embrace the process."

"Exactly so," she said, smiling, and went to sleep.

On another occasion she asked me what I thought Heaven was like. I said I would start by imagining what life would be like without having to drag around 150 pounds of living flesh that constantly needed to be fed and cared for. She was skeptical. "How would I know who I was meeting, and how would they know me?" she challenged.

"You would know," I said.

But she was not convinced. She wanted to make sure her friends and family would eventually be there in a way she could identify. She just could not imagine a life after death without all of you.

December 4

In response to my last e-mail update, a number of people have told me that they were aware of deceased relatives being ready to accompany newly dead persons on their journey, or of conversations between the dying person and people already dead (in Catholic theology this is called the "communion of saints"). At choir practice one Sunday I broke down crying over a particular song, and so we all got together and had a conversation about dying. Two of the choir members have had near-death experiences and corroborated the dark tunnel, the beautiful light, the accompanist, and the choice to go back. And they both remembered how beautiful it was there, and how they wanted to stay.

Often we don't feel comfortable talking about such events, but they are so common that I believe most people have experienced similar kinds of events at some point in their lives. For example, my friend Jeanne Finley related this experience to me:

> *The last section of your update reminded me*
> *of something that happened when my ex-husband*
> *[Sherwood] was dying, told to me by his new wife*

[Paula]. He was in hospice. He said, among other things, that he could see his parents very clearly, happily standing and waiting for him. (They had died several years before). It gave Sherwood much peace, because things had not been good between Sherwood and his father, and they had not made amends before his father died.

Soon afterwards I received a sequel from Jeanne. Out of the blue she had received a call from Paula, whom she had not heard from in a long time. Paula remembered the incident well and added this information:

Sherwood had not had any rapprochement with his father before his father died; but the parents were not particularly happy together in life for many years, to both of their sorrow...so for both of them to be there to escort Sherwood was quite revealing. According to Sherwood, his mother had said to him as she waited for him to die: "It's so beautiful here!" This is so amazing because Sherwood's mother was an avowed and committed atheist all her life, totally against religion and all that "nonsense," and had never believed for a minute that there was any kind of afterlife, or any god, or much of anything. So for Sherwood to hear his mother make that remark certainly suggests a "place," a heaven, a continued existence for all who pass.

December 13
Health update

Dear friends and family,

Wil's death seems to be approaching. She is too weak for visitors now. Fortunately her sister Maria has come from the Netherlands to be with her for two weeks, so I have very good coverage. I feel blessed and surrounded with love.

After my last update on Wil's health, about saying goodbye over Thanksgiving, a number of you took the opportunity to say goodbye in cards or letters. They were beautiful. Wil would come to me with tears in her eyes and tell me that I had to read a letter or card because it was so beautiful, and indeed they all were. I know Wil wanted to respond to these letters, and she had them out on her desk, but she just has not had the energy to do it. I wanted to respond to them also but have not had the time. So I want you all to know that your notes and letters were all read and appreciated. We would have responded if we could, but circumstances seem to have caught up with us.

Wil is now significantly weaker than she was. She said in the past that she wanted to live at least until her birthday on December 18, and there is a good chance she will make that date, but it would not surprise me if she died soon afterward. The signs are there. She thinks of all of you often, but realizes that now she must start to let us all go.

We have been having a series of conversations about her approaching death, which often overlap or are repeated. A composite of these conversations would sound something like this:

Wil: I am dying.

Steve: The health professionals don't think you will live more than a few weeks.

Wil: I am not afraid of dying. Really I am not. But I don't want to get lost after I die. Where am I supposed to go? Don't I have to prepare something? I want to bring my sewing with me, but what else? Suppose I get lost?

Steve: You remember all the near-death stories: the person goes down a long dark tunnel into this beautiful light and is met by beings in white robes or something like that—and in almost every story the person is accompanied. My friend was just telling me that a few days before her first husband died, his deceased parents became present to him in the room to accompany him. And when one of your clients in hospice died, he saw angels in the room waiting to accompany him. It's a very common occurrence. So don't you suppose that someone you know will come to accompany you?

Wil: Yes, I suppose someone will come to accompany me. But shouldn't I prepare something? What am I supposed to bring?

Steve: Well, you know the old story of the two babies in the womb. One says to the other, "I'm not afraid of being born. Really I'm not. But I don't want to get lost on the way out," and the other baby says, "I heard the doctors talking and they said we'll go down a long dark tunnel into this beautiful light and we'll be met by beings in white robes who will give us everything we need."

Wil: (laughing): That was a Henri Nouwen story about the babies, except you got it all wrong. He never said anything like that. You made that up.

Steve: Well, it's a good story, isn't it?

Wil: Yes, it is a good story. You think I should become like a little baby to die?

Steve: Perhaps it might help…Will you accompany me when I die?

Wil: Oh yes. I will be watching you from above, and when the time is right I will come and get you. You can be sure of that. Is it OK for me to go, then?

Steve: When the time comes to leave, you have to go. I will be OK down here.

This conversation, or a variation of it, gets easier every time we have it, but it still seems we are talking about something neither of us ever thought would happen.

Last night Wil was in a lot of deep pain. We tried different pills but nothing seemed to work. Finally she looked up and said, "The shawl." Our parish had given her a prayer shawl with the names of thirty-four people written on it, with their best wishes. I took the shawl and put it around her. She closed her eyes and concentrated very hard. After awhile I asked how she was doing. "I am concentrating on their faces and feeling their touch on me," she said. A few minutes later, I asked her again how she was feeling. "The pain is going away," she said, and fell asleep.

December 17

Announcement of Wil's death

Dear friends and family,

Wil died a few minutes after midnight on her birthday, Thursday, December 18 (by Dutch time), and a few minutes after 6 p.m. today, Wednesday, December 17 (by New York time). She was surrounded by our family and passed away peacefully without regaining consciousness.

Wil communicated to us this morning that she was not in any pain but was very weak and wanted to die. We told her that it was time for her to go. She took off her oxygen mask. Philip, Roger, Maria, and Shima were in the room. Margot had called that morning to say that she was sick and could not come from Maine, but she talked to Wil on the phone and sent a big bouquet of tulips. We took the tulips out of the vase and put them in Wil's lap. Then we waited expectantly, but she did not die.

We sang some hymns, ending with the song she wanted at her funeral, "When the Saints Go Marching In." She smiled and nodded her head in amusement. Then she said goodbye to all of us and we hugged her, but she still did not die.

Finally she told everyone but me to leave. I realized that it was very difficult for her to die with everyone around because we were earthly attachments holding her in this world. I sat next to her for awhile. Then her eyes opened wide and she said emphatically in Dutch, "It is finished."

I said, "That is good. You are on your journey, kid. Have fun."

She said, emphatically, "OK."

I got up and left the room to give her some space to die. But then Phil's wife Jill arrived from Washington, and Wil talked to her and did not die. She was frustrated, and said several times, "Why is this taking so long?" Eventually she gave up, put the oxygen mask back on, and had breakfast.

We all began a vigil that lasted until just after 6:15 p.m. Eastern Standard Time (12:15 a.m. Dutch time). Early in the afternoon she lapsed into a deep sleep. Late in the afternoon, Phil noticed that her breathing had changed, and we all went in to sit with her. Suddenly she took a deep breath. Maria and I looked at each other and nodded. I held Wil a little tighter, she took another deep breath, and she died.

Only later did we realize that she had died on her birthday, when measured by the country she was born in. She had said she wanted to die on her birthday, and perhaps that is why it took her so long, waiting for the change to the new day.

It might be more accurate to say that Wil had been dying all week. The language of death is rich, complex, and symbolic. Hospice notes that a dying person may say "I want to go home" when they are already in their own house, but the term "home" may be a symbol for something else. Wil's words during the week reflected this symbolic language.

Last week she began to spend most of her time in bed, often in a state that was not exactly awake but was not exactly asleep, either; more like a trance. Her eyes were closed and she was unresponsive to questions, but she was very active: her hands moved, her lips formed words. Occasionally she would say whole sentences out loud so that I had a sense of what she was thinking. And then she would drift off into real sleep. She appeared to be living in two worlds. I moved a cot into her bedroom and spent several nights next to her in case she needed me.

Saturday night she was in a particularly active trance. Her arms and lips were moving rapidly. Her face was furrowed and intense; she appeared to be in deep negotiations. At 3 a.m. she woke me up by banging around the room. I saw that she had taken her whole bed apart and thrown the pillows all over the room. "What do you think of this?" she said. "I am trying to build my case and I cannot find my attorney anywhere." She seemed agitated and worried and her face was lined with strain. I helped her back into bed and she fell asleep.

The next morning her demeanor had completely changed. Her face was relaxed and she smiled a big smile at me—like a litigant who had just won her case. Margot also noticed this remarkable transformation.

"What's up?" I said.

"My attorney...the case...the bell," she said.

"What bell?"

"You go three...two...one...zero...the bell."

"What bell?" I asked again.

"The bell to heaven," she said.

"You seem to be living in two worlds."

"Yes. The only thing I don't know is who will accompany me. It could my mother, or father, or Regina, or Sister Sylvia..." She went on listing friends who had died, ending with Father Daley, our old parish priest.

"Father Daley!" exclaimed Margot. "Did he die?"

"Oh no. I made a mistake," Wil said. "He is not dead yet. I just met him in the supermarket. He couldn't possibly accompany me. I must be losing my marbles."

Later she was still beaming, and told Margot, "Last night I passed over. Now the rest will be easy. The key to dying is patience." Hours later I asked her again about the attorney and the case and the bell, but she could not remember what had happened. All she could remember was a voice that said she had won her case. Nonetheless, the incident seemed to have had an impact on her, because she agreed to stop taking the salvestrols and vitamin C and appeared for the most part relaxed and calm.

My interpretation of this incident was that before Saturday night, Wil and I had been pursuing duel theories of seeking a cure through salvestrols and vitamin C while simultaneously preparing for death. But at some point you can no longer prepare for death while clinging to the hope of a cure. You have to decide on one path or another. We talked indirectly about this several times, but Wil was never quite ready to confront the issue head on and abandon the hope of a cure. Now death was staring her in the face, and she had to decide where she was going to put her trust. That, I believe, was the "case" she was arguing.

During her wrestle with the "attorney" something must have been disclosed to her—some "bell" must have rung—that convinced her that death held greater possibilities for her than her present life in her broken body. She came to embrace death and the new life it offered. This was the "passing over." Once she had accepted death, the actual dying part was "easy." It was just a matter of having "patience," and eventually this new life would be given to her.

There are skeptics, I know, who would say that all of this is simply the result of the morphine, which can trigger hallucinations and confusion. But I cannot help feeling that as death approaches, the veil that separates the two worlds becomes more transparent to the dying, like walking toward a carnival through a dark overgrown forest; light and music and movement from the carnival can be seen through the leaves, but its full shape and energy is confused and difficult to describe. The dying can see things others cannot, but when they try to describe them they sound "confused." Perhaps, in fact, it is the rest of us who are confused.

After Saturday's wrestling match with the attorney, Wil seemed to be spending more time exploring her new "home" without a body. On Sunday night she went back four hundred years to when Native Americans first met the Europeans. She banged around in the bedroom much of the night. She later explained to me that she was involved in these early meetings. She was particularly interested in the problem the Indians faced because they did not have a written language. What did they think when they saw that Europeans could repeat what other Europeans had said, when they looked at a piece of paper with lines on it? She talked with us extensively the next morning about it.

Because Wil had great difficulty talking, it is hard to reproduce her actual words from memory, but several of us commented that her tone and content were professorial and academic. She used a rich vocabulary and complex sentence structure that were quite unlike her normal tone of voice. ("And from this we can conclude that a synthesis of factors contributed to…"). It was almost as though she was channeling another person, as when the radio in your car suddenly picks up another station on the same wavelength once you drive out of range of the old one.

Later in the day she apparently visited a quilting friend in a trance. Because she occasionally spoke out loud, I could hear that she was instructing her friend on the correct way to value a quilt—what factors should be considered, etc. Again she used the professorial tone of voice.

Early Tuesday morning she was traveling in Alaska, and described to me (in non-academic language) the beauty of the icebergs. Later she and her sister Jos were sunbathing in California, and she was worried that Jos would get cancer unless she covered up.

On Tuesday, Philip and I were present when she asked, "Is everybody here today?" We responded that Margot was in Maine and would be coming back on Thursday. "Why isn't Margot here today?" Wil said. "I thought I could die today."

"You said that you wanted to die on your birthday, and your birthday is on Thursday, two days from now," I said.

"Oh," she replied. "Then I have to wait two days. I did not know I was that strong." While fully awake, she told Phil, "Tell everybody there is nothing to be afraid of. Don't be afraid."

Later, in a seeming trance, Phil heard her say in the professorial tone, "An (unexpected?) explosive event occurred in the creation of the universe that enabled our souls to have a physical presence on earth. We are all connected, and it will take time for all of us to restore the balance that the explosion disrupted. When you are born you get guidance on your…" Then, according to Phil, she stopped and turned her head toward an unseen person or presence in the room and said, "What?…Oh yes." Then she turned back and said, "…guidance on your journey." Phil immediately wrote down the words so he would not forget them.

Then Wil seemed to come out of her trance and said to Phil, "I can explain it better in a drawing." He brought her a pencil and paper and she drew two circles, one inside each other. On the circumference of the outer circle she made little dots, apparently representing individual personalities that had been driven out of the center by the explosive event. In the center she began to make many lines reaching out toward the circumference, trying to unite all of the dots again. She worked on the drawing for awhile until she was exhausted.

Then she said, "Eileen Caddy had a drawing like this in her book, can you get it for me?" Phil brought her the book and she opened it to the introductory page for the month of December. And there indeed was just such a drawing as she had been making. "Read what is written on the opposite page," Wil said. Phil read:

> *I was shown a great ball of light*
> *Coming from it were bright rays of light*
> *And going back into it were very dull rays*

I heard the words:
When you have been the full cycle,
you will return to me,
the source of all life,
and you will become one with me
as you were in the beginning.

Below this passage, Wil had written in her own handwriting at some earlier date:

And so I feel it will be.
Wil

This sequence of events leading to Wil's death may seem somewhat unusual, but I believe that they are really typical of what happens whenever a person is freed by death from the enormous limitations imposed on her by her earthly body. Wil may have been more outspoken about her newfound freedom than others, but I think it arises out of the same process of death that everyone goes through. It is for this reason that death is such a sacred and holy moment. It reveals, even for a brief minute, the immense power and love of the universe that is contained in each of us. As Tevye and Golde sing in *Fiddler on the Roof*, "It doesn't change a thing, but even so, after [a life on earth] it's nice to know."

January 10, 2015
Wil's funeral update

Dear family and friends,

Since Wil's death, a number of you have asked how I'm doing and whether I'm coping with the grief that inevitably accompanies the death of a loved one. I generally answer that I think I'm doing OK. But that answer condenses a lot of feelings and emotions into a single word, and that's not very helpful for you who are genuinely concerned for me. It also avoids the reality that the dying process does not end in death, but extends well beyond that. It's hard to know how I feel only a few weeks after Wil's death, because in a sense I'm still going through it. So I wanted to write one more update to explain all this, not only to you, my dear friends and family, but also to myself.

After Wil stopped breathing on December 17 I called hospice, and within a few hours they sent over a nurse to help prepare the body for its next journey. In the Netherlands, it is traditional for the immediate family to wash the body, and Wil had firmly told me that I was to continue this tradition. I thought her sister Maria, who was present when Wil died, would show me how, but Maria said it was a duty of the next of kin and she was not going to be present. So it fell to me, Roger, Philip, Jill, and the hospice nurse to actually do the washing and dressing of the body (Margot and her family were very sick in Maine at the time and simply could not come).

I have to admit that at first we were very tentative about the washing. Washing the body is an intimate, tender, loving act, and it takes some time to get used to, especially when done as a group project. But in the end, with the help of the hospice nurse, we were able to get Wil washed; Jill selected some nice clothes. We dressed her and laid her out on the bed. She looked very peaceful and almost youthful. The wrinkles of age and strain melted away on her face, and there was a Mona Lisa smile at the corners of her mouth. However, no matter how beautiful she looked in death, all of us agreed that washing the body was an important act because it made very clear to us that Wil was no longer in her body. Her body was still with us, but Wil had left.

We did not want to rush the body out of the house, and so we arranged for the funeral home to take the body the next morning. We decided to hold the funeral a week later so we would have more time to get organized, and after a lot of hugging and tears we all said goodbye and Phil, Jill, and Roger went home. Several days later, I drove Maria to Boston for her flight back to the Netherlands. Having Maria with us during Wil's last days was a great gift to me, and I was very sorry to say goodbye to her. She brought with her the love of all of Wil's siblings and their families in Holland, and she was a solid rock of care and good judgment.

The remainder of the time until the funeral is somewhat of a blur. Many friends and family members called and sent messages and flowers and food. The sense of love and concern and support was overwhelming to me. I wanted to personally thank everybody who reached out to me, but I soon realized that this was not possible at that time. The funeral had to be planned, the house made ready, programs had to be printed, and everything just blurred together after awhile.

I approached the funeral with some trepidation. I do not feel capable of organizing a cocktail party, much less a funeral, but once again (and this is a recurrent theme throughout this narrative) I was very fortunate to have three children and their spouses who were willing to do whatever was necessary to make arrangements, print programs, deliver eulogies, and organize food for the reception. I was fortunate that Wil and I had already discussed funeral plans, and I knew what she wanted. I was fortunate that we had interviewed funeral homes until we found one that we really liked. I was fortunate that Maria and Wil and I had discussed internment options and had decided together that we would bury half of Wil's ashes in Maine in my mother's plot and half in the Netherlands with her Dutch family. I was fortunate that Reverend John Kirwin agreed to do the funeral, because he was the most influential religious person in my life and knew Wil very well and could give me good advice and do a beautiful service. I was fortunate that Philip and others could devise a system so that the funeral service could be broadcast live to the Netherlands. Many of these funeral arrangements had been made before she died.

And I was fortunate that the funeral was held in our little church, St Francis in the South End. There are high churches, where a mighty God is enthroned above in glory, and there are low churches, where the Holy Spirit moves through the community and you look for the face of God in the eyes of your neighbor. St. Francis in the South End is the lowest church I have ever attended. After the service, the funeral director told me he had seen a lot of funerals, but he had never seen a funeral Mass quite like this one. If I had not told him, he said, he would not have been sure what denomination it was, but he thought it was very moving.

On the day of the funeral the church was completely full. So many people who had been important in our lives came from far away. I was particularly touched that members of different immigrant communities that Wil and I had worked with over the years were present. I alternated between joy and tears when I saw them. I regret not having time to talk intimately to each person who came, and apologize for this seeming insensitivity. But in the end I felt profoundly at peace with the service. I gave up all concern for the details, which I left to my children, and tried to stay in the moment and absorb as much as I could from the collective intensity of people's feelings for Wil. And, true to her wishes, we all exited the church with the chorus singing "When the Saints Go Marching In."

After the reception, the children stayed on at the house for several days to start to unpack decades of living that Wil and I had put together. Wil was very good at throwing out useless junk—as long as it was my useless junk. But she was unable to throw away anything that her friends gave her. It was all precious to her because her friends were all precious to her, and as a result the house was stuffed. And it is difficult to throw away anything now that might be important to the family, unless everyone in the family is present to say they don't want it (because their own houses are already stuffed).

Wil has left a rich legacy. First, she was a quilter, who every year for twenty years made quilts with her group that were donated to our church to raise money for the outreach center and soup kitchen. Over two decades, her quilting group has raised over $100,000 for the center, and in the process its members have woven themselves into a beautiful pattern of friendship. The basement is full of their fabrics and loving industry.

Wil was also an intense seeker of spiritual meaning in the world, and left bookcases full of books and ar-

ticles on religion and spirituality. She was also a devout
gardener and left a houseful of plants and pots and
shovels and all the equipment necessary to bathe herself in the fragrant soil of the earth. And because she
loved her friends and family so much, she left albums
of photographs and boxes of letters that she could never bring herself to organize or throw out. Miraculously, working together, the children and I cleared whole
rooms, even as they discovered long-lost treasures
from their childhoods that Wil had carefully saved for
them. It was very tiring, emotional, and wonderful.

In due course, hospice sent me a booklet on grieving, entitled *Healing Grief*. Like all of the hospice pub-
lications, this one was well done and told me what I
would learn if I spoke to the professionals. The basic
rule seems to be that everyone grieves the loss of a
loved one, but everyone does it in his or her own way,
depending on personality, the circumstances of death,
prior experience with dying, and other such factors
that can aggravate or mitigate the grieving process. A
sudden death is harder to grieve, and a violent death
even harder, especially if the person grieving was
somehow responsible (or believed he was responsible) for the death. All marriages that remain intact
must end with one of the partners dying first; the only
question is whether you are the surviving partner or
the dying one. But no parent wants to outlive his or
her children; the death of a child, especially a young
child, has a sense of someone dying "before his time."

On the other hand, the insight of the dying person about the dying process can be a great help for the surviving partner to grieve and heal quickly.

When I put this all together, I realized that I was again very fortunate. Wil had read extensively in spiritual books, had been a hospice volunteer, and had a deep faith; she led me through the dying process and taught me what I needed to know. Her death had been gentle, even beautiful. We had plenty of time to prepare for it together. So I found that many of the aspects of grief described in the booklet, including anger, guilt, depression, and silence, did not resonate with me—at least not yet.

I did have one experience with anger that stayed with me in part because it was so bizarre. In October, when Wil was starting her final descent to death, a polar vortex swept out of Canada and dropped a killing frost throughout the Northeast. I awoke one morning to find that all the flowers in Wil's garden, which had been blooming so lustily the day before, were now just frozen corpses. A sudden anger sprang up in me—which, if I could put it into words, would go something like this: *You stupid flowers! You knew the frost was coming but you just bloomed your heads off as if nothing would happen. Look at all the effort you wasted. You thought you were so beautiful and precious, and now you're as dead as if you'd never made any effort at all. What was the point of that? What possible good did you accomplish?*

At some point in my rant against the flowers, I became aware that I was not really talking to the flowers. Having exhausted themselves by blooming, the flowers presumably were happy taking the winter off to rest up for spring. (They live within the cycles of the seasons, while we try to escape the cycles of death and rebirth and are always disappointed when our escape attempts fail.) But the rant raised some questions in my mind, which a pamphlet about grieving was not equipped to answer. What was the point of Wil's life, or any life? Why was it necessary to crush a beautiful flower like Wil who was blooming so exuberantly? If Wil was no longer in her body, where did she go?

A friend gave me a short book, *A Grief Observed* by C.S. Lewis, about the death of his young wife from cancer and his painful grief. (Her death was made into a movie, *Shadowlands*.) The book suggested to me that people who need a great deal of control in their lives find death particularly infuriating because there is no way to control it. If you view your loved one as your "possession," then God has taken your possession from you and there is no way to make Him/Her give your possession back. For some people, grieving may require that they wrestle with God in this way. People grieve differently, and I respect these differences. However, there are other ways of looking at death.

All through Wil's dying process the thought that comforted me most was that death was natural. We don't have to hold anyone responsible for death; rather we have to understand how life and death are connected and part of a continuum. Death is not so much an end, like a black hole, but is more about change—extreme change, perhaps, but change nonetheless. We know from physics that energy is neither created nor destroyed but can only be changed from one form into another. The energy in falling water can be changed into electrical energy in a turbine, which is changed into heat and light energy in a light bulb. Are we not perhaps something like that?

I am not talking here about reincarnation, where the same individual is supposedly reborn over and over again. Reincarnation is a nice theory, but it gets too complicated for my comprehension when people try to explain how the same individual is reborn, but with the mind erased, so that the earlier life is forgotten. I am only suggesting that people change after they die. I have no idea whether they are reborn or what that would even mean.

I had my first suggestion of "death-as-change" as a teenager when I read Shakespeare's *The Tempest* in high school English class. My father died during World War II in a diving accident. I was three years old at the time, but he was mostly away at the war; I have no recollection of him, and I grew up without feeling any personal connection to him. I was in class reading *The Tempest* when suddenly there appeared these lines:

*Full fathoms five thy father lies. Of his bones
are corals made.*

*These are the pearls that were his eyes. Noth-
ing in him that doth fade,*

*But doth suffer a sea-change, into something
rich and strange.*

*Sea Nymphs hourly ring his knell; Hark!
You can hear them—*

Ding Dong Bell.

My mouth dropped open. The Bard had described
my father. True, he had described my father as "something rich and strange," which wasn't very helpful; also
the Navy had recovered Dad's body, and he was buried
on land in Saratoga Springs, so his eyes had not literally
become pearls. The poem was metaphorical, as the language of death is metaphorical. But it got me thinking
about Dad, and where he was, and what he expected of
me. I wondered if he expected me to go into the armed
forces, or perhaps avenge his death in some way. I finally decided that if Dad were asked, he would say that
he wanted me to be happy and enjoy a rich and full
life that had been denied him. And this belief became
deeply rooted in me. Of course, one couldn't just say
"I want to be happy" and presto, one was happy, but it
helped to think that whenever I was happy, I was helping to justify the sacrifice that Dad made.

When I was in my early 50s, our men's group at
church went on a retreat centered around the theme

of fatherhood. During the course of the weekend we talked about our fathers and shared the wide variety of experiences of fatherhood. At the end of the weekend, we were invited to stand in a circle and say something to our fathers. When my turn came, I said, "Dad, until I became a father I did not appreciate the sacrifice you had to make when you died. Being a father has been the most wonderful thing that has ever happened to me, and so now I can feel how much you lost when you could not be with us as we grew up." Then I realized that those were the first words I had ever spoken directly to my father. I went into the parking lot and sobbed for fifteen minutes. When I returned, I told the leader of the group, "That was the first time I ever cried about my father's death." He gave me a wry look and said, "Well, it's about time."

After that, whenever I went past Saratoga and had some extra time, I would stop off at Dad's grave for a chat. They were friendly, peaceful talks, not very profound. But they helped to build a relationship. Gradually I came to believe that Dad had always been with me and had helped guide me through some of my more difficult periods. I just had not realized it.

The point of all this is that I approached Wil's death with some sense of how death changes people, and how in changed form the deceased can begin and maintain relationships long after death—even fifty or more years after death, in my father's case. My Aunt Betty, who died at age 108, used to joke that she would return as a butterfly. Shortly after she died, Roger and Meredith were married at a beautiful outdoor ceremony, and right in the middle of it a big beautiful butterfly flew in and hovered over the couple. My family gave a collective gasp: "Betty has arrived!" They also had this sense of death as change. I think feeling the presence of the deceased in nature is very common, and that many people have experienced it.

Before she died, Wil planted over a dozen amaryllis bulbs indoors in pots. By the time she died, none of them except one showed any sign of blooming, and I put that one on the mantelpiece. On the day of the funeral, however, that amaryllis suddenly burst forth into glorious bloom—eight large flowers, and four more came later—twelve in all out of just one bulb. I had never seen such exuberant blooming, and I felt I knew who was responsible for it. Also, on the day after the funeral I received an e-mail from a prospective client asking me to come to Pakistan (at her expense) for a meeting about representation of one of the wrongfully convicted terrorists whose cause I had earlier advocated. It was as though Wil were saying to me, "See—this blooming amaryllis is a sign that I passed over safely and that I am still with you. I know you took nine months off from your civil rights work to help me in my illness.

Now it is time for you to get back to work again. I give you permission." At least that's how I intuitively interpreted the flower and the e-mail.

Is it just a coincidence that at the time of the funeral only one out of many amaryllis bulbs flowered extravagantly, and that I was offered a chance to go to Pakistan to promote civil rights? Of course it's a mere coincidence. Coincidences happen all the time. It must be a coincidence...unless....it's not. And the possibility of Wil's continued spiritual presence and communication charges my life with a special excitement and sweetness. Her spirit may still with us. She and I might still be partners in living.

When someone dies, we can preserve her memory with photo albums, biographies, special events, ceremonies. Christians preserve the memory of Jesus in the communion ceremony of bread and wine, which itself commemorates the exodus of the Jews to freedom. But the essence of life is dynamic, humorous, changing, active, and reactive. The Church also recognizes this in the presence of the Holy Spirit, the dynamic religious wild card that knows no boundaries except love. (One can argue that the Church actually tries to suppress the Holy Spirit into something it can control. We can't have universal love breaking out all over: the Catholics and Episcopalians might start worshiping together, and God knows what would happen after that...but I digress.) So in this context, it seems perfectly normal to me that Wil's spirit would visit me and would continue to inspire and animate my life, as though she were alive.

In the end, the only important question is how I, the surviving partner, combine different elements in order to lead the richest, fullest life possible in the time that remains to me. Arguing with a cruel God, or dwelling on memories of lost happiness, seem counterproductive. But if I should make space in my life for the dynamic spirit of Wil, or my father, or a host of other friends and ancestors who have gone before me, I see no harm in that—only a richer and fuller life.

Henri Nouwen, in his book *Our Greatest Gift*, points out that everyone who goes through a process of dying essentially goes through a process of becoming a child again—both dependent on and innocent of what is to come. Fruitful dying is not dying alone but instead dying in solidarity with everyone who has ever died before or who will die in the future—which is literally everyone. Such a fruitful death enriches us with hope and spirit for generations to come. Nouwen answers my rant against flowers that froze to death by suggesting that in their death, they left a richer environment in which future generations could grow. And in this respect, humans are not different than flowers.

Nouwen tells the story of a terminally ill friend who went to Lourdes looking for a miracle cure. When she came back, she told Nouwen that she saw all the

sick people at Lourdes who were about to die and realized that she did not want a miracle that would save
her alone; instead, she wanted to die in solidarity with
all of them. "Solidarity" here means recognizing our
common bond with all of humanity. In a better world,
all people would die with justice instead of oppres-
sion, with peace instead of violence, with love instead
of hatred and conflict. To affirm this, even in our last
hours, is to fertilize the soil for the next generation to
grow an even richer harvest of love, justice, and peace
to be shared by all. We do not have any choice as to
whether we will die, but we do have some choice as to
the message that our death will send. Fruitful dying
is a community event at which our spirit is shared,
broken, and consumed for the benefit of all.

This, then, is the last and best gift Wil gave to me
while she was alive—a death we experienced together in peacefulness and love, and which left me (and
her friends and family) a legacy of faith and hope for
the future and empowerment to live as fully as possible in the time remaining. Wil read Nouwen's book
thoroughly before she died, and she underlined this
passage as perhaps her final message to me:

> *Will our death give new life, new hope, and*
> *new faith to our friends, or will it be no more than*
> *another cause for sadness? The main question is*
> *not how much will we still be able to do during*
> *the few years left to live, but rather how can we*

prepare ourselves for our death in such a way that our dying will be a new way for us to send our and God's spirit to those whom we have loved and who have loved us.

Epilogue

In April of this year, all thirteen members of the Downs clan—the families of Margot, Roger, and Philip, and I—went to the Netherlands to spend time with Wil's Dutch family, have a memorial service, and scatter half of her ashes on the 200-foot "mountain" behind the town of Goor where she was born. We arrived a few days before the service, and quickly divided our family up so we could all stay for a few days with several Dutch cousins. It was wonderful to see how quickly even the youngest children on both sides recognized that they had special relatives who did not share their language, but with whom they had a family bond.

On Sunday we all met in Goor for a memorial service at the church. Wil's whole Dutch family was there, as well as many of her friends. Family members expressed how important she had been to the family and how she had influenced their lives, and remembered adventures they had experienced in America as children while visiting our family. When it came my turn to speak, I said, in part, the following:

I love this church. Wil and I were married here in 1968. I remember kneeling right there by the altar listening to the ceremony in Dutch. At one point all eyes turned to me. Wil, realizing that I did not speak Dutch, banged me with her elbow, and I exclaimed, "Ya. Dat belof eek!" ("I do")…and I was married. It was the happiest day of my life. So it seems appropriate that we should all come back to this church to complete Wil's life with a memorial service.

When I married Wil, I always understood that my greatest competitor for her affections would be Goor. She grew to love America. She was insistent that part of her be buried with me in the U.S. But I would have felt uncomfortable if we had not brought part of her back to Goor to remain with the people and the land that she loved so well.

In saying this, I sound as though we have divided Wil up—half to the Dutch and half to the Americans. But I can assure you that Wil would not have thought of it that way. She would have said that she was uniting her American family with her Dutch family so she would never have to choose between them. The family would always be one, no matter which side of the Atlantic they were on. To prove the point, we have brought all of her American descendants with us to this service so that they will all get to know their Dutch cousins and our family will never be divided.

*I feel that her spirit is still with us and with
all those who knew and loved her. Henri Nouwen
talked about a fruitful death, in which a person's
death enables future generations to live deeper,
more spiritual, and more enriched lives. So it is,
I believe, with Wil.*

At the end of the service we exited the church clapping and singing "When the Saints Go Marching In," as Wil had wanted, and we all lined up for a group photo (which is included in the centerfold of this book) outside the church—the first photo made of her whole family still living. Then we went to the top of the Herikerberg, the 200-foot "mountain" that she'd loved so much as a child and where my children had played when they came for visits. After some readings and prayers, it was time to scatter the portion of her ashes I had brought with me to the Netherlands.

I had never seen scattering done, and nobody I'd ever talked to had seen it either, so I just made up a protocol for how to do it. There was a clear patch of forest downwind from where I was standing, so that Wil's ashes would blow across the cleared land and fertilize it. I felt that scattering was a joyful, energetic act of freedom, and so spontaneously I began to run back and forth upwind from the cleared patch, letting her ashes blow out of the jar and across the forest. When I saw there was just a little bit left in the jar, I threw my hands into the air in a triumphant gesture of liberation and watched her last ashes swirl away into the wind and disappear. Wil was free. I did not know whether to laugh or cry, but I saw that the others felt the same way, and so we hugged each other and laughed through our tears.

We spent the rest of the week visiting with our Dutch cousins. Wil has five younger siblings still living, and most of them have spouses and children and grandchildren, for a total of about forty individuals. All of them have been good friends and family to me and shown me much hospitality over the years. All of them are unique and interesting people with wonderful stories to tell. I wish I could describe each of them here.

In being with my Dutch family, I had a strong sense of being with Wil. She had brought me to Goor, introduced me to her family, and told me stories about them and about the town. She had shown me the city center that had been bombed in World War II and the secret places she had played in as a child. We'd biked the little paths through the fields to the castles that were located just outside of Goor and played with the kids in the woods on the Herikerberg. We had been back to Goor many times, but this was the first time I had been there without Wil. I realized that wherever I went, I was seeing the people and places through her eyes, and that whatever emotions I felt were those we had shared. It was almost as though we had become one.

Back home, our family (and friends who were really family) gathered together again on July 11 at a little cemetery in Southport, Maine near our summer home and laid to rest the other half of Wil's ashes, in a grave that I intend to share with her when the time comes. The service was very informal and focused on having the youngest generation, ranging in ages from two to ten years old, feel comfortable with both their grandmother's death and her continued presence in their lives. (The grandkids called Wil "Oma," Dutch for "grandma," so she would not be confused with my mother, Elinor, who is "Omi.")

Wil and I had decided to have the phrase "Bloom where you are planted" placed on the gravestone, and we had talked about what this phrase might mean. When she was alive, Wil talked about her need to bloom in this strange, exotic land of America into which she had been transplanted. But now that she was dead, the phrase took on a slightly different meaning. We would be "planting" a container of her ashes in the earth like a precious flower bulb. What kind of a bloom might we hope for in the years to come?

The grandchildren seemed to understand the beautiful mystery of this question. They all helped cover Wil's ashes with earth; the eldest played a melody on her cello; two others sang "Let It Go" from the Disney movie *Frozen*, a favorite song of Wil's when she was dealing with cancer. One of the youngest said, "I feel Oma in my heart." The second-eldest observed, "Oma was the flower. When she finished blooming, we became the seeds from that flower, and we will bloom too."

The question of how Wil will bloom in the future is really the same as Henri Nouwen's idea that death can produce a fruitful harvest so that the influence of a person's life continues long after her death. We cannot choose to avoid death, but we can choose what influence, what blooming, what fruitfulness our death will have. Wil's body has now been cremated, scattered, and interred, but her spirit is free to be alive in the world and grow the harvest of the future.